Mary N. Balcomb is a designer, etcher, and art writer who lives in the Puget Sound area. She graduated from the American Academy of Art, Chicago, and has a BFA *cum laude* from the University of New Mexico and an MFA from the University of Washington. A contributor to *American Artist* and *Southwest Art* magazines, she is author of *Nicolai Fechin: Russian-American Artist*, and *William F. Reese: American Artist*. As a member of the (USA) Author's Guild, she has foreign and domestic design projects to her credit. Balcomb is an advocate of the arts for all children and is a founding member of the Children's Arts Foundation, Inc., Seattle.

Balcomb's work is represented in collections in England and France as well as in the U.S. Exhibits include solo etching shows at the Frye Art Museum and the Nordic Heritage Museum, Seattle.

Her etchings are called intaglios (in-TALL-yo -- "below the surface") which is one of the oldest art forms, dating to the incised images in Paleolithic caves and in the later engravings of knights' armor, the drypoints of Rembrandt, the aquatints of Goya, and the line etchings of Whistler, Winslow Homer, Picasso, Mary Cassat, Kaethe Kollwitz, and other masters.

Because of her love of drawing and her drawing abilities, the intaglio, particularly line etching, carries a special fascination and is her natural metier. She etches her own plates and does her own printing.

With Best Wishes,
Mary N. Balcomb

ROBIN-ROBIN

A JOURNAL

Drawings and text by
MARY N. BALCOMB

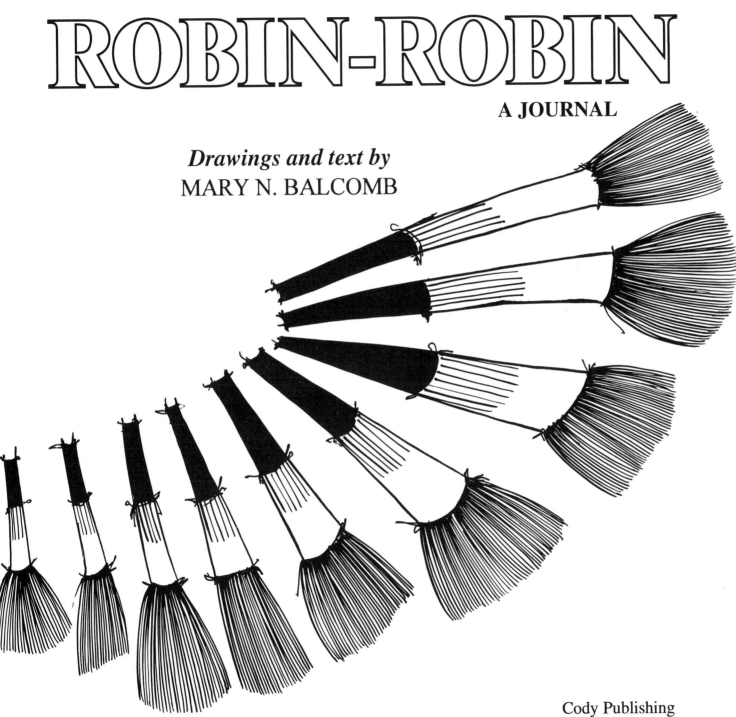

Cody Publishing
Seattle, Washington

ROBIN-ROBIN : A JOURNAL
First Edition
Copyright © Mary N. Balcomb, 1995
(Text and all illustrative material)
First published in 1995 in the United States of America
by Cody Publishing
3213 N.E. 94th. St.
Seattle, Washington 98115

Design, etchings, drawings, photographs: Mary N. Balcomb
Studio photographs: Robert Balcomb

Library of Congress Cataloging-in-Publication Data
Balcomb, Mary N., 1928-
      Robin-Robin : a journal / drawings and text by Mary N. Balcomb. --
   1st ed.
         p.   cm.
      Includes bibliographical references.
      ISBN 1-887532-06-4 (alk. paper). --
      ISBN 1-887532-05-6 (pbk. : alk. paper)
      1. Robins--Washington (State)--Puget Sound Region--Biography.
   2. Robins as pets. 3. Surrogate parenting of a wild bird. 4. Art-Etchings, drawings,
      and photographs of a robin's development.   I. Title.
      QL696.P288B34 1995
      598.8'42--dc20
                                                                95-22236
                                                                     CIP

This book is dedicated to my husband Sam,
who raised ROBIN-ROBIN, and to my
mother Selma, who loved and enjoyed
the remarkable little bird.

Special acknowledgements:
To Dave Pearson, whose tremendous
effort and expertise – and gentle
prodding – made a printed prototype of
ROBIN-ROBIN: A JOURNAL *a reality.*
To the many friends, especially
Irmgard Bruser, Nat Kaplan, Sue and Bill Hurd, and Amis Balcomb,
Imy Klett, Fran and Bill Reese, and Elizabeth Tapper,
who have faith in me and my work.
Thanks, too, to Sharon Pearson, Dennis Fahlen,
Fred Madrid, Zina and Joe Hurd, Jorgene and Johanna Giovanelli,
Devin Nolet, Jane Lotter, Tessa Marts, Barbara Iliff, Ethan Brotherton,
and Bich-Thuy Le and Holly Eberhart.

Illustrations:

All illustrations are reproduced from original etchings drawn and printed by the author unless otherwise noted. Photographs are by the author and her husband.

Cover: Robin-Robin (etching).
Frontispiece: "Hope" Four blue eggs (etching).
Title Page: Robin-Robin's "Paint Brushes"(pen and ink drawing).
Back Cover: Author with Robin-Robin (photograph).

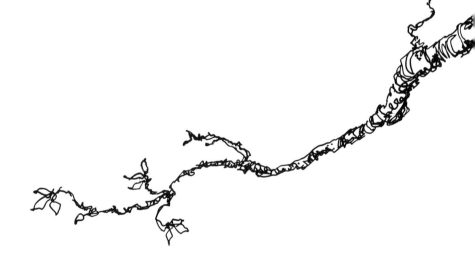

Contents:

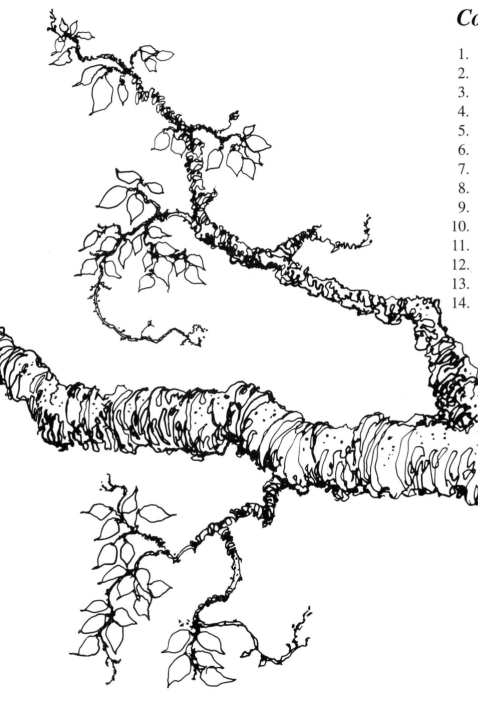

Note: Because this is an artistic journal to educate and entertain, the artist-author has purposefully strengthened certain lines in the photographs to show Robin-Robin's anatomical features more clearly.

" . . . The tameness of birds provides not only pleasure but also a problem of remarkable interest, the selection of which may well assist the better understanding of the behavior of mankind."

David Lack
The Life of the Robin

Location, Location, Location

"Maybe they've gotten their seasons mixed up." What else was one to think? It was mid-December, yet the trees against our bedroom window had burst forth like pink popcorn. But this wasn't Florida or Southern California, it was the Pacific Northwest -- latitude 47° -- and we already had snow, although admittedly it wasn't much of a snowfall and the winter thus far seemed milder than those we had experienced in New Mexico in prior years. A neighbor quickly set us straight: "They're winter-blooming cherries."

Fifteen seasons later, my husband Sam and I continued to exclaim about the unorthodox, lovely blossoms that greeted us each gloomy winter's day -- pink petals that glistened in the rain or gently emerged and disappeared through the fog. The blooms lasted until early March before succumbing to rapidly growing new green leaves. For awhile cats and squirrels frolicked or had frenzied races using the trees as convenient links between our roof and the ground. Gradually the squirrels disappeared and then most of the cats, except for one or two neighboring toughs. Not once in all those years had any bird even considered the cherry trees as a possible nesting site.

13

Yet one day in early May of the sixteenth spring, a robin couple began sitting in the trees, conversing noisily. First they sat on one limb and then on another. It became a daily ritual with excited dialogue, always in the same volume. Then they were gone. We didn't see them for several days and assumed they had found another, more suitable place; but one day Mrs. Robin reappeared with a beak-load of moss and sticks.

She alighted on the upper fork of the tree closest to the window, affixed the materials to the thick "Y," and left. Soon she was back with another load. She worked and worked, weaving the sticks and then stuffing them with mud and moss. She made a wide, solid base on which she constructed vertical walls until she had an open cup, a structural hemisphere.

When the exterior was finished, she brought fine, soft dried grass for the lining, tamping it meticulously with her beak. Next, she went slowly around and around the nest, stopping at short intervals to lower herself onto her chest, enabling her to push or tamp the walls horizontally backward with her feet. Only her beak and tail were visible along with the busy action of her feet. What was an amusing sight to us, a robin lying on its stomach kicking its feet, was serious business to her. As a final touch she butted the whole interior with her body. All in all she worked 12 to 14 hours over a period of four days. Then she disappeared.

A fifth day came and went. No robin. On days Six and Seven, still no robin. On Day Eight she came momentarily, as if to inspect the project, and then disappeared again. Sam and I realized that she was letting the nest dry before she moved in.

What puzzled and annoyed us was that never once during the building process had Mr. Robin shown his beak. Why had he let her do all the work? It was obvious she hadn't needed him; she knew exactly what to put where and knew how to get the job done. However, it would have been gentlemanly if he had brought in a few twigs just to help her out. Maybe he was miffed about something. Perhaps they had disagreed on the layout of the nest or the proximity of it to our window or about the number of children they should have. Or maybe she figured that it wasn't any of his business. After all, SHE was the one who was going to live there, so she might as well build it just the way she wanted.

Move-In Day

Day Nine arrived and, as was our usual practice upon waking, we checked the nest. She was in it! Apparently she had made another inspection, found it to her liking, and had moved in; but she seemed restless, as if uncertain about something. Too much moss on the bottom? Not enough on the sides? She stood up. She crouched down. She stood up again. Back down. Then she shifted counter-clockwise about 45 degrees, but that didn't seem to suit her either. She stood up for the third time and then turned in the other direction. Soon she leaned close to one edge, then farther, until her feathered breast hung over the side.

She was all puffed out. In fact, her whole body appeared enlarged and her head seemed tiny in comparison, pulled close to her "shoulders," turtle-like. Moments later she began breathing hard; her chest was heaving and her eyes were somewhat glazed, staring, other-worldly. She was preoccupied and for a brief interval, unconcerned with the world in general.

"She must be laying an egg!" Sam said in excited but hushed tones.

We had never witnessed such an event before and because we weren't up on bird lore, we didn't know for sure what we were observing; but we knew it was some sort of phenomenon. Whatever it was, it was a palpitating, exhausting effort for Mrs. Robin. She was either laying an egg or having a stroke. We waited. In a minute or two she appeared more alert, stood up, turned around, and looked at the bottom of the nest. She probed at something at her feet and then lowered herself into the nest slowly, gently, until only her head and tail were visible.

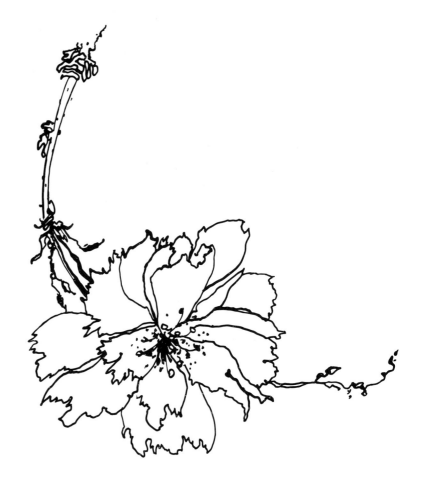

We still couldn't fully appreciate the drama which had just occurred before our eyes. Was there an egg or not? We had seen birds and bird nests all of our lives, but they were obscure, out of reach, high above our heads in the tree tops or rafters. Each year barn swallows built and rebuilt their nests on the roof beams inside our carport. Tell-tale signs on our cars announced their arrival in the spring, and for the duration we parked in the driveway; then after some weeks when we and our cat were no longer being dive-bombed, we knew the birds were gone, and that was that for another year. These were passive experiences. We never timed or observed them more fully; we were certainly never privileged to a grandstand seat such as we had now. It had all been quite impersonal.

Mrs. Robin's situation was different. Since the nest was at our eye level, not four feet away, we were aware of all her comings and goings. We could not have ignored her if we tried.

Now, we kept an especially close watch. One of us kept a constant vigil, reporting every movement in muted tones to the other. After an hour, when she finally left the nest, we were ready to investigate. Sam contrived a periscope by taping my compact mirror to the end of a broom handle. He opened the window and cautiously eased the contraption toward the nest -- both of us nervous about Mrs. Robin's possible sudden return. Finally the mirror was positioned over the nest -- Lo and behold, one beautiful blue egg! We stared at the reflection of the miracle and glowed; we had witnessed something wonderful. No longer was this an ordinary nest, nor was she just any old robin. We became possessive. She was OUR robin and soon there would be babies to enjoy. We became protective: How were she and the babies to remain safe from nest robbers and other mishaps?

While we were envisioning doing battle with the tough neighborhood cats, robber crows, blue jays, and other enemies, Mrs. Robin returned. For the rest of the day her behavior remained normal. She was in and out of the nest on a schedule of sorts: in for 30 to 40 minutes, off and away for 15 to 30 minutes. Once she was gone for a full 45 minutes and we began accusing her of negligence. We assumed that if she allowed the egg to become cold, it wouldn't hatch. How dare she be so careless with our baby.

At 11:30 the following morning she began to puff out again and went through the same ordeal as before. And so did we. Then, when she left, we found a second egg, just as beautiful as the first. She lay two more eggs through the following two days, stopping at a clutch of four.

Incubation brought stronger commitment to the nest. She allowed herself the rarest absences for food, sitting on the unsheltered nest in blazing sun with beak open or toughing it out in cold rain. One day a mild spring shower turned into a torrential driving rain, then to hailstones. I made numerous nervous trips to the window to see how she was faring. She was crouched low to provide a drier, warmer cover for the eggs; only her head and tail were visible, but the unusual posture of the head, one which I'd never seen before, made me race to find Sam.

Four beautiful blue eggs.

"Come! Come quickly," I shouted as I ran through the house. Sam dropped what he was doing and came running as fast as he could. I whirled around two steps ahead, half-yelling, half-gasping as I ran, "You'll see a sight that you've never seen before and probably never will again!" His mind raced, not knowing what to expect. As we crunched through the doorway, I vigorously waved my arm toward the window. He could see poor Mrs. Robin on her nest drenched with rain, pummeled by hail. Upsetting as it was, the situation of itself did not seem to be the problem I had built it up to be. However, it was harrowing to witness the wretched bird being bashed about under our very eyes. We stood glued to the window, helpless, staring at her. As we watched we both began to realize that it was truly a phenomenon. She had turned her beak skyward almost 90 degrees, thus offering less surface for the stones to hit; but the marvel was that she had spread tiny hair-like feathers, which grew on the upper base of her beak, into an arc and fanned them out over her nostrils and eyes (like a car windshield visor but upside down). Mother Nature had thought of everything -- not only a program for living, but instincts for survival with back-up systems.

Mrs. Robin kept her eyes partially open, protected by the "fan," until it began to hail again. Then, seeming to grit her teeth, she pointed her beak even higher and closed her eyes completely. The hail pelted her relentlessly until she was covered, a mountain of stones on her back and a white ring around her nest. It looked as if she were taking a bubble bath, but without the pleasure of it.

We hoped for a halt in the storm, worrying about such things as Mrs. Robin over-heating under the

Mrs. Robin turned her beak upward and braved the storm.

20

blanket of ice or the ice melting sufficiently to congeal so that she wouldn't be able to free herself. But these were ridiculous worries -- finally, the hail storm abated, Mrs. Robin slowly rose, breaking the mound of white pebbles, stood up, shook herself off, repositioned her stubborn little body on the nest, and continued her job.

How long would it take the eggs to hatch? None of our bird books gave us information about the lives and habits of birds; they were mostly concerned with identification and migration. Months later we found David Lack's *The Life of the Robin*, John Terres' *Songbirds in Your Garden*, and Austin Rand's *Ornithology: An Introduction*, and my mother gave us *That Quail, Robert* by Margaret Stanger. Lack says the incubation period is from thirteen to fifteen days, and generally only the hen incubates. We also learned that the eggs are soft-shelled when laid and gradually harden with exposure to air. Birds turn or roll their eggs to maintain an even temperature within them to develop the embryos and to keep them from settling and sticking to the shell; but "the hen does not start incubation until the clutch is complete." [1]

Geraldine Flanagan and Sean Morris, in their discussion of blue titmice, say that hens who lay ten or twelve eggs, one per day, have a method of delaying development until all the eggs have been laid, by deserting them daily instead of keeping them warm. According to the authors ". . . the inborn 'delay switch' against immediate incubation prevents the first-laid from becoming too advanced over the others. Otherwise, the first two or three hatched would have such an advantage in size and abilities that this would have ruined the chances of survival for the later younger ones." [2] The size of the species determines the size of the nest and the number of eggs to be laid, which then generally determines when incubation is to begin.

In our case, Mrs. Robin seemed to start incubation right away. Her babies hatched on subsequent days so that the first one was actually four days older than the youngest sibling, explaining the smaller size and weakness of the last compared to the others. It became obvious that even one day makes a whopping difference in the life of a baby bird. Why hadn't Mrs. Robin waited until the fourth egg was laid? Was she new at the game, anxious to start her family, anticipating a trip in July, or did she simply want the whole business done and over with?

Studies on robins show that they lay three to five eggs, although English robins, which are smaller in size, have been known to lay ten. How did those mothers ever manage? Square footage in the nest is at such a premium and feeding a mob like that must be an awesome task, especially if the father is as lazy as our Mr. Robin -- who hadn't even offered to help with the nest. (We really were disgusted with him and wondered if he was going to put in an appearance after the babies hatched. We chastised him thoroughly.)

Further information from Lack made us retract our words when we read ". . . in most song-birds both sexes build the nest but in the robin only the hen builds. Sometimes she chases the cock away (who occasionally wants to help)." [3]

The New Family

When the babies began to hatch, Mr. Robin did appear. The poor dear had stuck around all the time, ready and willing to assume his share of the responsibilities, apparently just awaiting approval from the Missus. One evening we observed them as they both stood on the edge of the nest surveying their new off-spring, an intertwined indistinguishable moving mass of naked, reddish, scrawny, blind nestlings. Not a pretty sight to human eyes, but probably a most beautiful one to the robin couple.

Soon the parents had an assembly-line feeding program going so that we decided not to spy on the babies anymore for fear that one of the parents would collide with our periscope. It was amusing to see one stuffing the frenetic gaping mouths while the other was in a "holding pattern" waiting for clearance to land. Birds masticate food for the newborn, and it is thought that this process provides necessary enzymes for their development. As the babies grew older, their meals of insect puree became more solid: whole grubs, worms, beetles, and dragonflies, long legs and all.

Dozens of bird families in our ravine, maybe hundreds, were going through the same routines. Each day began at four in the morning, songs and chatter became more and more voluminous as the season progressed and little voices became stronger. Sometimes it was almost deafening -- but wonderful! Twenty or thirty minutes later all was hushed again until 5:30 or 6:00, a time which seemed to suit Mrs. Robin better. She did not rise with the others* but stayed quiet and in bed as long as she was able. Heaven knows she needed the rest because from then until dark her responsibilities never ceased -- it was one load of groceries after another. She never had a chance to sit with her feet

*Generally it is the males only who sing, proclaiming their territorial rights while the mother birds tend their young.[4]

Four cavernous orange mouths opened at the slightest sound.

25

propped up, much less to think of the empty-nest syndrome. Perhaps when she was pulling her tenth worm of the day, she prayed, "Please, let the sun set early tonight." When night did come, she carefully positioned her feet in the nest, settled down, and dutifully spread out her feathers to cover her babies and the opening of the nest while Papa slept on the edge or on a nearby tree limb.

Was this the same couple we'd seen in the area for several years? Was this the same cock who kept attacking our living room windows for two years in a row? That particular robin had used the same strategy over and over as he approached our windows: first, he flew to a branch on a cedar tree, then to a higher one on the same tree, and then down onto a springy fir limb just a foot away from the window. As the branch swayed up and down with his weight, he bobbed his head up and down in the opposite direction to keep it exactly level, all the while keeping a steady eye on something inside. It was as if his bouncing body were suspended from his head with rubber bands. Then, just at the right moment, he hurled himself at the window and clawed it vigorously, claws raking the glass as he lost altitude. When his feet hit the sill, he sprang backward, catapulting into flight.

The household, thinking that was the end of the episode, went back to its quiet routine. Not fifteen minutes elapsed when the peace was again broken by another thud and more scre-e-eching on glass. Surely, by now he should realize the barrier was impenetrable -- but soon he was back, lunging at the window with full vigor. He came with such force that he lost small feathers and body fluids which blended with his dusty imprints into wavy paths from his claws and made an awful mess.

Why did the robin behave in this manner? Was there something in the room that caused his aggression? There were no birds or animals, live or otherwise, in the room -- perhaps he didn't like the orange sofa -- or perhaps he thought it was his dear mum reincarnated. Not only did his persistence shatter our nerves but we thought he might injure himself. We finally realized we had to discourage his bizarre behavior, and feeling like monsters (guilt-ridden about our behavior) we pretended to counter-attack from inside. It worked.

It wasn't until later we learned that robins are territorial and fearlessly fight for their spaces, a back yard for example. The male robin drives away intruders, especially other robins, by puffing up his breast, displaying it threateningly. The "enemy," unsure of himself on foreign ground, scares off. If he does not leave, Cock Robin takes stronger measures and fights -- even an "intruder's" reflection in a picture window!

Lack's information on color-ringing of birds showed that ". . . all, or almost all, of those male robins which have once established territories are thereafter non-migratory."[5] (The oldest robin recorded up to that time was eleven years old.)

Our babies were becoming larger, stronger, less transparent, and more vocal each day. They began bobbing and stretching their necks on the third day. Their chattery heads shot up to unbelievable lengths at the slightest sounds and out of their cavernous orange mouths came a chorus of speeded-up chirps, each pleading a hardship case for its own stomach. They fidgeted and shoved and shuffled constantly during their waking hours. In just a week's time the nest seemed too small. How could they possibly have managed with even one other nestling? Obviously Mrs. Robin had done some planning.

If all the fates are with them, baby robins remain stuffed in the nest for about twelve days. Then they either fly or fall out. The parents continue to feed them, following them from pillar to post with beaks loaded with food. Lack says that some fledglings begin picking up food about the eighth day out of the nest (twenty days after hatching), but frequently the parents continue to feed them until the forty-first day. This is why it is not uncommon to see a parent stuffing food into a baby who appears to be twice the size of sparse Mom or Pop.

Parenting continues . . . and continues.

Family Crisis

Content that we still had a week or two to observe the development of our babies, one can imagine our shock when we awoke to an empty nest on the morning of June 3. What had happened? The babies weren't old enough or strong enough to leave, nor even sufficiently feathered to stay warm. But, there was the nest, VACANT. Had a raider come in the night or had the babies simply shuffled themselves out of the nest? We ran down the stairs several steps at a time and carefully searched the tangled ivy beneath the tree. The morning air was disturbingly still. Nary a peep. Not the annoying brattle of the jays, not even the distracting, threatening sounds from the parents who generally raised a ruckus if man or beast neared their babies. It was as if a mass exodus had occurred. In our disbelief of such an event, we continued to pick our way through the ground cover, gently turning over leaf after leaf. The search ended about fifteen feet away from the tree when we found the regurgitated remains of two baby birds.

"It was that monstrous cat," I muttered, not daring to raise my voice in case the other babies were alive and nearby, "that miserable, murderous beast. I hope it choked on the rest." We continued probing the grounds but found nothing more. Sadly we returned to the house cursing the tailless cat with the bulldog shoulders, the "grey menace" who hissed at our cat through the sliding glass doors.

Minutes later, I heard Sam racing down the stairs again, slamming doors as he went. He had examined the nest with the periscope and found a single baby cowering at the bottom. Then apparently it mistook the quick image in the mirror as its parent or maybe he thought the Night Terror had returned -- something spurred the little thing into action, catapulting him over the edge of the nest, plummeting him to the ground. How long had he been huddling alone and unattended in the abandoned home? Where were the parents?

Sam found the baby in the ivy. It was still alive, and it opened its mouth; but Sam, remembering old tales, was afraid to pick it up for fear the parents would reject it if they did come back. He came into the house wondering what to do next -- he knew he couldn't wait too long -- birds have such a high metabolic rate that they must feed frequently or starve. And the baby was still so lightly feathered that it could die of exposure.

We waited. We took turns at the vigil, sufficiently well hidden not to frighten away the parents, yet at the ready should the Gray Menace reappear. Neither friend nor foe came. Sam finally went out, dug around for an earthworm, and with a pair of forceps offered it to the little orphan, who accepted it ravenously. Well, that did it. No more dalliance. Sam brought the bird in and put him in a cardboard box lined with facial tissues and placed it on the workbench downstairs.

He bent his beaks back practically double
as he yelled for more.

A New Mom and Pop

The little thing had wing feathers of sorts with suggestions of more to come. The head was as good as bald except for two rows of down branching in several directions, resembling fuzzy moose antlers. A trail of down followed the spine to where tail feathers would eventually be. His armpits, sides, and bottom were bare and reddish -- he certainly looked unfinished -- and pathetic. He sat in the box on his bare bottom, supported by scrawny, pale grey elbows. Stomach temporarily satisfied, he pursed his lips and went to sleep.

Sam's search for worms began in earnest. We had to have a supply ready for the next feeding in fifteen or twenty minutes. He scoured the yard: two worms, a juicy spider, and a dragon fly. "That should be enough for three or four meals," he announced with great satisfaction -- pleased with his own resourcefulness.

Sam offered the worm first and his little charge practically bent his beaks back double as he yelled for more. He accepted the spider's abdomen but not the legs, and he refused the dragonfly; however, he was still hungry. Not until that moment did we realize we were in real trouble -- not another worm or insect could be found; numerous frantic inspections of the yard proved fruitless, making it obvious that we were seriously deficient in some aspects of bird parenting . . . WHERE had Mr. and Mrs. Robin found all those worms?

"I'm going to have to go to the sporting goods shop to buy worms," Sam finally admitted, a bit chagrined by his failure as a provider. He made a hurried trip, bringing back six-dozen worms.

"This surely ought to be enough for a couple of days. They certainly are EXPENSIVE! They charged me $2.40 -- let's see, that's over three cents a worm!"

Robin ate gluttonously every twenty minutes or so and each time, after he had his fill, fell asleep almost immediately. (I was able to observe his eyes and realized for the first time that the bottom lids moved upward to close -- opposite to human eyelids.) At the end of two hours he had made a tremendous dent in the worm supply; if we didn't make another run to the sport shop before it closed, we'd be in a mess of trouble. This time Sam approached the salesman with, "Look, I've got this problem," and he proceeded to tell about the baby who was eating us out of house and home. "If it's going to stay with us for two or three weeks, I can't afford to keep it in worms at forty cents a dozen," he pleaded.

The salesman took pity on him and sent him to the worm farm where he would be able to buy worms at wholesale. For eight dollars, Sam bought three one-quart cartons of worms, and he was happy in the thought that at last he had a proper supply.

"They'll store nicely in the refrigerator," the worm farmer assured him.

Robin finished the first batch of worms and started in on the new supply before he went to bed that night. The next morning he opened his mouth wide as Sam offered him the first breakfast worm; but as the forceps

He clamped his beak shut and refused to open it again.

neared, he clamped his beak shut and refused to open it again. No amount of coaxing could make him open up. Sam waited and then gently nudged his beak, to no avail. He kept trying, sometimes clacking and smacking his lips, attempting to convey the deliciousness of the meal, but the bird would have nothing to do with the eight-dollar worms.

"Swell," Sam muttered, and said some other indistinct words. "Now, what do we do?"

Robin certainly wasn't full. We could tell by his crop, a storage chamber below his esophagus which became swollen and distorted as Robin would stuff himself. The food would remain there to be softened and stored until the stomach could accommodate it. Maybe the bird was sick? Things went from bad to worse -- he began to lose his vigor -- we were frightened that we would lose him. We searched for help in the telephone directory, looking for an Audubon Society number but finding nothing, then we called the County Humane Society. Luckily, they were able to give us the phone numbers of people who care for injured and homeless birds.

"Don't be too disappointed if he doesn't make it," the first woman consoled us. "Many times the birds do well for two or three days, and then they have a delayed reaction to the shock they have experienced. Perhaps this is the case with your bird."

Her disheartening suggestion seemed to hint at the symptoms of Robin, all right, but we did not wish to yield to such thoughts and asked her for instructions for his care. She gave us a full regimen: feeding, watering, bathing, nesting, and expected behavior. The diet consisted of high-protein foods: ground meat, beef heart if possible, baby cereals mixed with boiled egg yolk and enough water to make a paste, and Terrell's Red Label canned dog food.

Drinking water was not necessary until later because the food contained sufficient moisture. She also suggested a cereal bowl lined with crumpled paper towels to serve as a nesting cup.

"Give it a tree limb, too; otherwise its feet will atrophy," she said. "And you must keep the baby warm -- put a 25-watt light over the box.

"Oh, and another thing, dip some of the food in clean, unsprayed dirt or sand. That'll help the bird grind its food."

Sam sped to the store a third time. The beef hearts were so large that he settled for a half-pound of ground round instead. In the meantime I boiled a few eggs, and the bird's banquet began to take shape. When it was all set, Sam tempted the baby with cereal-and-egg-paté. To our surprise, coaxing proved to be totally unnecessary: we had managed to pique his appetite. Next came the ground steak, and the little glutton almost swallowed the forceps. Our motherly, baby-stuffing instincts were overflowing with satisfaction. We glowed with success and happiness.

We began our own assembly-line feeding program, but soon discovered that Robin required less in quantity, possibly because the quality was better than the full diet of worms. We learned much later that less than half of a robin's diet is animal matter, principally insects, with less than 10% worms, while the remainder is made up of small fruits and berries. No wonder he had clamped his mouth shut -- he had simply O.D.'d on worms.

Robin spent a good portion of that day and the next in the cereal-bowl-nest (in the box). The tree limb, placed next to the bowl, was of no interest to him because he

He was still sitting on his elbows.

was still sitting on his elbows. Sometimes he relaxed so completely that he actually dozed off and lost his balance. Each time he righted and rearranged himself, only to doze off to repeat the same act again. Because robin babies are well packed in their nests, they remain upright by mutual support as they doze in unison. It must be a secure feeling.

But our poor baby had such a loose arrangement in the cereal-bowl-nest, even with the crushed paper towel lining, that he must have had a sensation of falling into infinity, which caused his rude awakenings. In retrospect, had we known better, we would have provided a tighter nest, a basket with two or three lamb's wool companions for warmth and security.

Robin was fastidious about his nest. Even from the first day in the roomy cardboard box he managed to back into one corner or another to use the bathroom. He pushed his bottom as high up the corner as he could in an attempt to find the edge of the box; but, of course, the sides were too high and the discharged droppings landed half-way up. This behavior puzzled us at first; then we realized that he was trying to drop his waste outside the nest. We marveled at his inborn tendencies, the instinctive patterns, uniquely programmed within each of his kind. The nesting bowl was a definite improvement. He began to sit on the rim which enabled him to drop his discards outside his bedroom and thus fulfill his innate housekeeping needs. We had observed his parents tidying the nest when the babies were new, by carrying away their droppings in their beaks.

Settling In

At first we handled Robin minimally. He had come into the house involuntarily in the palm of Sam's hand, but if he was apprehensive, he didn't show it. Neither did he appear to mind being picked up when we cleaned his box. In fact, he seemed to like being nestled in a cupped hand. Thus, we took advantage of his good nature and began to hold him more and even started photographing him at various intervals. We were nervous about using flash bulbs -- and didn't -- as we gently manipulated him to record his anatomy.

JUNE 5. The great, wonderful bonus today is that Robin VOLUNTARILY "discovered" Sam's index finger and wouldn't let go! It was the clinching act. From then on we were helplessly enslaved by a little bird. Neither one of us would be the same again. Robin grasped our fingers with his toes and tiny claws -- WHO could resist such a gesture? This voluntary touch from the pure and innocent melts the gruffest of us -- we interpret it as affection, or at the very least, a show of friendship -- we do not stop to question or analyze whether it is a natural reflex, or a function, or a necessary act. In Robin's case, maybe he instinctively hopped on the finger to flex his toes (which he did unceasingly) and then didn't quite know how to let go. Anyway, it has become a pleasurable daily habit. Soon, he found the tree limb, too, and abandoned the cereal bowl for good.

JUNE 6. The V-shaped bald spot on the crown of Robin's head is filling in with minuscule feathers, and his body feathers are becoming more evident; but his wings still look as if he were an advertisement for paint brushes. He is attached to dozens of tiny tufts of hair with white plastic handles! He nibbles at them and tries to flap each wing, and

He discovered Sam's finger.

as he does, he sends a blizzard of flaky debris from the erupting "plastic" tubes. He even tried to scratch his head, which was quite a trick because he hasn't developed sea-legs yet; however he bravely stood on one wobbly leg, pulling the opposing wing down, and maneuvered the other leg up, behind, and over the wing in order to scratch, before he lost his balance. He persisted and eventually mastered the technique. In our ignorance, we thought he was pursuing fleas, but Rand says:

> The growing feather emerges from the skin as a dark, blood-rich, pin-feather with a grayish, scaly sheath. New material is added at the base and the tip is pushed out. As the feather grows, it bursts the sheath, which flakes off as the vane expands. A grown, dry feather is in effect a dead structure; material cannot be added or withdrawn by the physiological processes of the bird. Damage by wear or breakage is not repaired.[6]

Robin's box is beginning to be too confining. He has tried several times to get out, but he couldn't negotiate the sides. Rather than risk having an injured bird, Sam placed the box on the floor so that Robin wouldn't have far to fall. And, because the bird still isn't fully clothed, we fastened a dim light to the side for warmth.

JUNE 7. Today Sam decided that Robin is FEMALE. The breast feathers, now more prominent, are pale and speckled.

"So-o I think he's a SHE," he announced.

He looked like an advertisement for paint brushes.

The feather grows from the base and not from the tips as do most plants, and emerges through an opaque tube (sheath) which is partially filled with blood for nourishment. As the feather pushes out and flattens, the tube splits open.

39

Her voice is stronger and she has started a ritual of communications. She remains quiet until she hears Sam's step on the squeaky stairs, usually about 6:30 A.M. Then she begins a series of insistent chirps but pauses between each one to listen for a vocal response from Sam. As he nears the door, she increases her volume and becomes an absolute shrew by the time he reaches her. She expects her food instantly. And she wants it jammed far down her throat. Undoubtedly the forceps remind her of her parents' beaks.

Robin's box has now been placed on its side, and she has free access to the shop floor. Her legs are stronger, and it will be good for her to be able to hop around. They are changing color: from a milky gray to a reddish brown. Her long, thin claws are sharp as they open and close against our fingers. We have noticed for the first time that she has segmented toes with textured toe pads and padded "palms" on her feet -- they are unbelievably like our hands, although instead of the linear pattern of our finger prints, Robin's feet have a pebbly texture.

"I wonder if each bird on earth has an individual toe print," I remarked.

Her stance is considerably more upright, and she is totally dependent on her feet for support, rather than her elbows (or maybe they should be called "knees").

Later in the day, Robin exercised her new-found freedom by following Sam around the shop, occasionally hopping on his shoe if he paused at his tasks. If he forgot and moved too quickly, she fell off. Undeterred, she bounced right back and hopped as fast as she could to catch up with him again.

He is attached to dozens of tiny paint brushes.

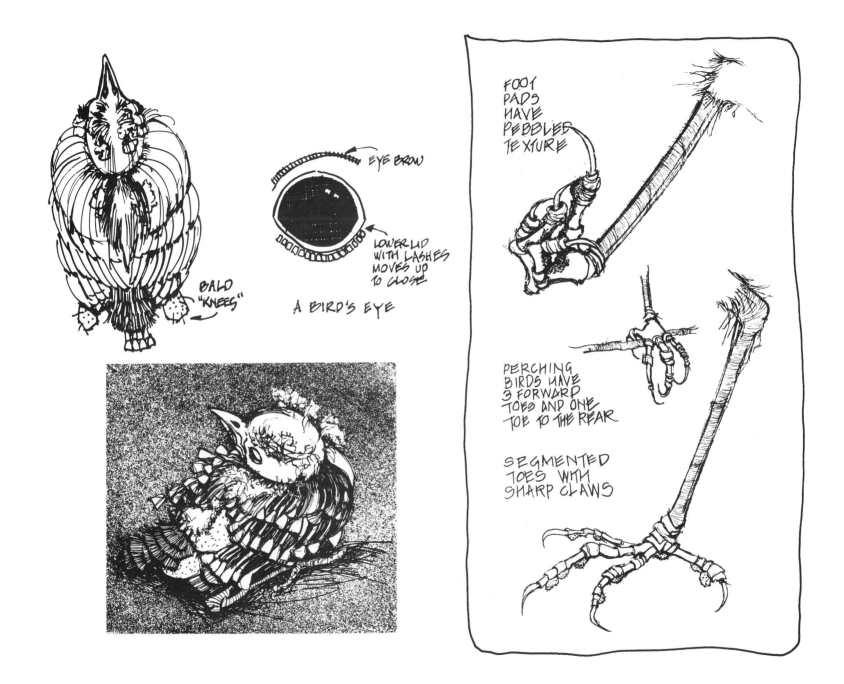

BALD "KNEES"

EYE BROW

LOWER LID WITH LASHES MOVES UP TO CLOSE

A BIRD'S EYE

FOOT PADS HAVE PEBBLED TEXTURE

PERCHING BIRDS HAVE 3 FORWARD TOES AND ONE TOE TO THE REAR

SEGMENTED TOES WITH SHARP CLAWS

JUNE 8. The dialogue between man and bird is becoming more complex, at least on the part of the bird. Sam's part is limited to clicks and clacks of the tongue and to one kind of whistle: soft and short, to which she has a "social" response. But she has a variety of sounds which signify her needs or moods: greetings, alarm, discontent, demands for food, and the contented muffled crackle sound when her tummy is stuffed -- almost like the purr of a kitten.

The afternoon was sunny, and we decided that Robin was ready to join us on our deck. It just didn't seem right to keep her where she couldn't see the light of day (our shop had been a photographic darkroom and the windows were still covered with blackout material). Besides, she was gregarious and loved Sam's company. She accepted me, too, but she really preferred Sam. We put her on the deck floor several times, but each time she just stood huddled in the one spot on which she was placed. She was but a speck on a vast floor, and the world overwhelmed her; furthermore, the wind was a bit on the chilly side. Sam scooped her up and she nestled contentedly in his cupped hand. She remained that way all afternoon, except for her many lunches, while Sam read. We had brought her kitchen to the deck, so the paté was only an arm's reach away.

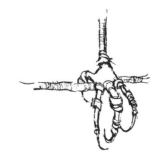

The dialogue between man and bird is becoming more complex.

On one occasion I found Sam sitting low in his chair, his chin practically on his chest, sound asleep; and Robin snuggled against his palm, sound asleep, too! What a wonderful sight. I would never have believed it if I hadn't seen it with my own eyes.

Partners sound asleep.

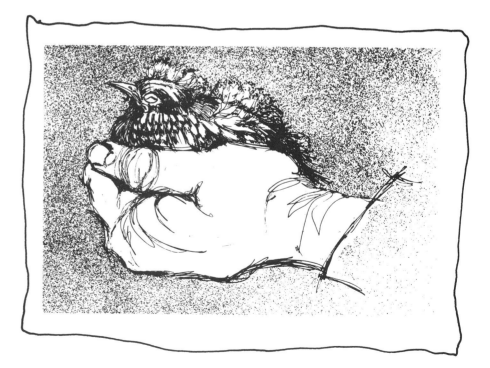

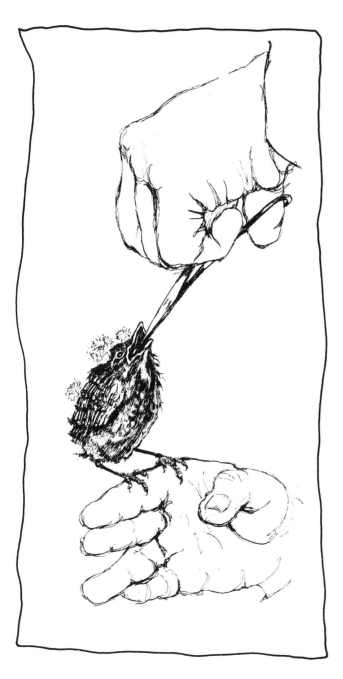

Paté ala forceps.

The Joys of Parenthood

JUNE 9. Robin has even more volume today as she scolds Sam through the door for not hurrying with her breakfast. He has learned to open the door cautiously because she waits for him directly on the other side, resisting every nudge of the door. When he finally manages to coax it open and has physically appeared, Robin makes a beeline to her dinner table at the opposite side of the room where she shrieks and stamps her feet. She is impatience personified.

She has no interest in taking her food from Sam's fingers but insists on paté-ala-forceps and gorges until her whole front is massively misshapen. We tried periodically to tempt her with the eight-dollar worms but she always stubbornly shut her beak. After being very badly snubbed, the worms are now living happily in our old compost pile.

Robin is blossoming out into a regular beauty with a full head of feathers and a covered bottom. The gray, downy underwear next to her skin is there for insulation, while the coarser vaned feathers on top will keep her dry in wet weather and will give her a streamlined form. Joel Carl Welty in his *The Life of Birds* says, "By actively sleeking, fluffing, and ruffling its body feathers, a bird can to a degree maintain its optimum body temperature despite external temperature changes."[7] Robin did seem to be fluffed out at times, especially when she was relaxed; but when she was excited or running, she was compact and sleek and looked considerably thinner.

Robin began sitting on our shoulders, at the nape of the neck, and on Sam's head. Her tiny claws tickled and raised goose bumps on us. Because she was so close to our ears, we could hear and feel every sound she made -- cherkles, crackles, burbles, gargles, peeps. She was a sheer delight. Terribly distracting -- but what a joy. We didn't seem to accomplish anything other than the basics in our own lives and sometimes not even those. Well, what did it matter? This was a once-in-a-lifetime experience. How many other people can claim to eating lunch or to reading with a Robin on the shoulder? And, bird droppings on the collar?

We had read *That Quail Robert* and envied how well-trained she was; not so with Robin. Nothing was predictable. We did learn to wear old clothing topped with a barber's cape or an old towel; and we always had a roll of paper towels handy. How DOES one train a bird to the social graces?

On head, hand, shoulders . . . Robin enjoyed it all.

Author's mother and companion.

47

JUNE 10.   Concern about Robin's future surfaced every so often. What was to become of her? When will she be ready for her freedom and will she be able to cope with it? Anxious to do the best for Robin, Sam called the bird woman again.

"Don't release the bird until it is able to feed itself -- not until it can find its own food -- and, not until its tail feathers are at least two inches long," the bird woman advised. She also suggested taking it to the state park, away from neighborhood cats, when it was ready to go. We silently envisioned the day of departure, imagining ourselves in a darkened, wet forest, waving good-bye to our helpless, unworldly baby -- no one to snuggle her in a cupped hand, no shoulder to ride on. IT WAS TOO MUCH TO BEAR.

"Well, for one thing, the tail feathers aren't anywhere long enough," we reasoned and quickly put aside all thoughts about releasing her.

Sam introduced Robin to a Pyrex pie plate containing an inch of water. She knew immediately what to do with it, hopping in with uninhibited glee. She scooted down, dunked herself over and over, and flapped her wings vigorously, splashing water for several feet in all directions. When she finally finished her gleeful plunges, she spent the rest of the day preening.

She still isn't able to fly upward more than two feet. In order to reach the top of the work bench, for example, she must do it in stages: first, she flies to the shelf on a roll-around cart, then to the seat of a drafting stool, and then from there an easy hop to the bench top. She makes a few joyous, teetering pirouettes before her next practice flight back to the floor. This cycle is repeated until she is exhausted or until she spies a new object that must be examined.

What was to become of her?

JUNE 11. Sam hesitantly placed Robin on the lower limb of the apple tree in our front yard, not fully knowing what the consequences might be, but she sat quietly for over an hour while he read the newspaper nearby. Then she rode out to the mailbox on his shoulder, an activity she prefers next only to eating and bathing. She seems especially attracted to Sam's blue shirt, so he wears it for her nearly everyday. I have to wait until he goes to bed in order to launder it -- well almost.

We have known for some time that birds do see color, but hadn't realized that they have preferences. Welty confirms this in his information on color experiments with birds. For example, he discusses the placement of colorless objects against various colored backgrounds: the objects which received the most pecks were those shown against green or yellow -- the premise is that the colorless objects took on the PREFERRED colors, red or blue (within the bird's brain as in man's), when placed against their complementary colors of green or yellow. Interestingly, too, robins and blue throats have shown an obsession for removing objects which match their own orange or blue plumage, explaining why Cock Robin is especially disagreeable when another robin enters its territory.

Rand's evidence, too, reveals that birds see color much as we do and in fact probably in a more advanced way: "Indeed, it has been suggested that certain oil droplets colored red, orange, and yellow which occur in the cones of birds' eyes may enable the birds to distinguish mixes of pigmentary colors to an extent possible to man only with the aid of filters."[8]

What a beauty she is!

50

While "The eye of the bird has reached a state of perfection found in no other animal,"[9] "... the bird's hearing range is not much different from ours."[10] How, then, are birds able to hear worms in our lawn and we can't? Is it because their ears are closer to the ground? Or do they have some kind of sensory element in their toes? (Right now, our Robin doesn't care anything about the lawn or what might be in it.)

She was three or four ounces of fluff making impatient demands on her human parents.

The Terrible Two's

JUNE 12. The morning dialogue began at the usual time, Sam again opened the shop door slowly, cautiously, for Robin still can't understand that in order for Sam to appear the door must swing open; but her logic seemed to be that if one wants something, one must move toward it, not away -- quite reasonable! Therefore she stood as close to the object of her desire as possible, and it frustrated her to be pushed away. Continuing to nudge the door gently, Sam felt no resistance. As he opened the door wider, there was no little greeter. Instead, she was sitting on the workbench. When Sam was fully in the doorway she chirped and FLEW to greet him! It is a distance of about twelve feet, and she didn't quite make it to his outstretched hand. She landed unceremoniously in the food dish he was holding. Pride in her achievement helped maintain her dignity and overshadowed her misplaced landing. She rode victoriously on the mountain of egg paté as Sam set her and the food dish on the floor. Hopping off almost before the dish touched down, she ran like a streak to her station on top of her chosen box and began stamping her feet for breakfast.

Her habit is to stand on this particular box, stamp her feet, give impatient double-whistle-chirps, and flutter her wings in between each bite until she is satisfied. How wonderful self-confidence is -- a mere three or four ounces of fluff on toothpick legs, putting on a big act by stomping first on one foot and then the other, twitting, and making demands to a six-foot giant who could crush her with his little toe! She had learned early how to make him "heel" -- all the cuddling in the palm of his hand and the gurgling and cooing in his ear -- what an easy pushover he was.

Frequently she eats her meal in three stages: first, on her box; next, on her limb on the shelf of the cart; and finally, in a niche on the shelf itself, where she then begins preening after the last mouthful. As Sam was following her from box to cart to shelf with forceps full of food, I reminded him about the mother robins we had seen, beaks loaded, running around the lawn after their young (and about the human mothers we have known following offspring with a spoonful of vegetables). But, he shrugged it off good-naturedly and continued to pamper the little one.

Sam also gave Robin a shallow box with soft earth in which she is beginning to spend a surprising amount of time pecking at things. Occasionally she picks up bits of gravel and swallows them.

She sat for her first formal portrait today. A photogenic and obedient model, she posed on a section of tree limb brought in expressly for her pleasure. What a beauty she is!

JUNE 13. Robin flew to greet Sam in a more ascending angle. Grossly over-shooting her mark, she tried to make an emergency landing on top of the door frame but it was too narrow. She lost her balance, yet somehow managed to turn around and in the split-second process gained enough momentum from the spring-board action when she touched the frame, to enable her to make a return flight toward her food station. However, she landed on a sloping piece of cardboard and went skiing off the end, plummeting to a crash landing on the floor. As if vexed, she ran back to Sam and began shredding the newspaper under his feet.

First formal portrait.

She bathes daily now with great gusto and even sips her bath water, which is changed (if any is left) after every bath. A good portion of each day is spent in preening, removing more broken sheathing, and oiling her feathers. An oil gland at the base of her tail enables her to spread the oil to her feathers with her bill. Welty suggests that because of the complex structure of feathers, they need considerably more care than skin or hair.

As witnessed earlier, Robin, like other alticial birds, did not grow feathers uniformly over her entire body, but in certain areas called feather tracts. First, the down feathers in sparse tracts, then hair-like filoplumes next to the body, and then more and more layers of protective contour feathers. Longer, stronger (contour/quill) feathers on the wings and tail as they mature will enable Robin to fly with more swiftness and grace. She still has downy antlers on her head and back, swaying and fluttering unmanageably, comically, as she capers about.

Sam moved her tree limb into the studio and photographed her again. She is an excellent though untidy model.

She stre-t-c-h-e-s and tests every moving part many times each day.

JUNE 14. Robin continues to eat with her usual vigor and frequency. She tolerates the dogfood, but loves the ground round and the paté. She had her first strawberry from the garden and gobbled it up in a few bites. The other robins are enjoying the berries, too. My first impulse was to shoo them off. The berries had been ripening for over a week, but I had yet to taste one. Each evening I pegged several which would be just right for our breakfast, relishing the glorious taste in my imagination, only to awaken each

She stretches and tests every moving part.

morning to find mere shreds hanging from the hulls, or no ripe berries at all. I had tied up the plants to keep them away from the slugs, not realizing that the berries would be at the birds' eye level. What a perfect set up! They didn't even have to bend down to eat.

But somehow I just couldn't shoo them away. Things were different now that we had a robin of our own. Instead, we looked the other way. What did it matter if they ate every berry that ripened! "To know is to protect" never seemed to be more true.

William Finley in *Birds of America* takes this position about ripening fruits and berries:

> In view of the fact that the robin takes ten times as much wild as cultivated fruit, it seems unwise to destroy the birds to save so little. Nor is this necessary for by a little care both may be preserved. Where fruit is grown it is no great loss to give up one tree to the birds; in some cases the crop can be protected by scarecrows. Where wild fruit is not abundant, a few fruit bearing shrubs and vines judiciously planted will serve for ornament and provide food for the birds. The Russian Mulberry is a vigorous grower and a profuse bearer ripening at the same time as the cherry, and, so far as observation has gone, most birds prefer its fruit to any other. It is believed that a number of these trees planted around the garden or orchard would fully protect the more valuable fruits.[11]

In retrospect, we had more than enough berries. The robins had had their fill after the first bearing and didn't bother with the fruit after that.

Another Crisis

JUNE 15. Sam went down the stairs with the first breakfast of the day. As he approached the door, he wondered what antics lay ahead this time -- he had not heard a sound from Robin. It was too quiet for comfort. He opened the door with his usual care but again noticed a lack of resistance; more unusual, however, was the absence of fierce scolding. Gone were her scathing chirps about his slowness and negligence. Gone, too, was the tongue-lashing about her poor, starving body. No sound. No motion.

"Uh, oh, what is she up to?" he puzzled. "Maybe she'll surprise me with a new flight pattern." He flipped on the fluorescent ceiling light and found Robin perched on an unused chandelier, placed there for storage. She seemed to be caught unawares. Scrambling from her perch, she started to fly toward Sam but lost gliding power instantly and fell to the floor with a thud.

She was glassy-eyed and shaking limply. Was she having a stroke? A heart attack? Had her demise come despite all our care and attention -- or because of it? Maybe we had been over-attentive, feeding her too much? These and a dozen other questions ran through Sam's mind. Instinctively he turned off the overhead light and switched on a lesser one; sickness and death seem more appropriately dealt with in softer light.

As he stood helplessly over the prostrate bird, wondering what to do, how to help her, she began to revive. Seemingly shocked by her prone position, she bolted upright and began to run. To Sam's surprise, she quickly resumed her normal activities including a multitude of sharp reprimands about her late breakfast. It was as if nothing had happened. In fact, she was peppier than usual, went through all her tricks, had a gloriously wet bath, played and ate all day, and still wasn't ready for bed when 8 o'clock rolled around.

What had been her problem this morning? She obviously had not heard Sam approaching, and perhaps he had been quieter than usual; but this didn't seem sufficient reason for her bizarre behavior. We worked backward from the incident: the chandelier, the fluorescent light, the door, the outer li-gh-t -- that was it! That had to be it. Sam had not turned on the outer-room's light. Thus, no light had streamed in under her door, neither to forewarn her nor to enable her to adjust her eyes to the sudden burst of the glaring fluorescent. Of course -- she was overcome! The shock from total darkness to instant daylight stunned and disabled her; it was hardly the way Mother Nature introduces her day.

When Robin finally went to bed, she did so with a small, yellow darkroom safelight which Sam had installed near the chandelier. The dim light became the symbol for night, her moon. From then on it was her signal to fly up to the chandelier to roost. And, never again did Sam forget to turn on the outer light.

JUNE 16. Sam filled a second shallow box with wet earth into which he dug a dozen worms from the compost, and casually laid it on the workroom floor. Not too impressed, Robin stared at something in the box now and then, tilting her head as if to zero-in with just one eye, but mostly she ignored the whole thing. However, a check at the end of the day revealed that the worms were gone!

"Why, the little scamp," Sam grinned. "She knows what her beak is for -- how to find her own food -- yet she has us waiting on her hand and foot."

We knew we should be elated with this discovery, with her progress, but we also knew that with every new step of self-sufficiency we were closer to losing her. Again we chose to dismiss the thought.

She had quite an active day, including two baths and a good introduction to Bing cherries, which she loved instantly. At 8 o'clock when we turned on her night light, she flew to her roost; but she then flew right back down again. She was full of mischief and wanted to play. However, she had worn us out and we were ready for a rest; but before we went, we decided to open the blackened but screened window to let in the warm night air (it was the first time the temperature had been high enough to enable us to do that). I felt guilty about leaving Miss Sociable flitting and hopping about the floor so I went down to check on her again at 9:30. She was perched on the window sill forlornly staring out through the screen into the darkness. When she saw me she flew and alighted on my shoulder, something she had never done before.

"She MUST be lonely. Even MY shoulder is acceptable now," I mused. Naturally, I stayed a while. . . .

JUNE 17. Robin posed for additional portraits. Two fluttery down-feathers remain on her head and several on her back. A couple of tail feathers are still encased in the plastic tubes. Her baby imprint, the touch-sensitive whitish flanges around her mouth, have all but lost their curvature. She enjoys having her beak stroked. I wonder if it, too, tingles with growth.

Robin posed for additional portraits in our studio.

A Show of Independence

JUNE 18. We took Robin out on the lawn again. She pecked at a few things in the grass but, as usual, she stayed close to the retaining wall and just sat. What would her life be like in the wilds? Would she make it? Or had we domesticated her to the point of dependency on us? If that was the case, couldn't we build a large aviary, to include our front lawn, and keep her forever? We couldn't bear the thought of parting with her and tried to find new excuses and justifications for keeping her. (A fact we didn't know at the time, was that all songbirds are protected by federal and state laws, except English sparrows and starlings. If you raise these birds, you may legally keep them, but other wild birds should be allowed their freedom after proving they are capable of caring for themselves.)

JUNE 19. Although Robin rides around on Sam's shoulder and on his index finger without flying off, she is more independent in attitude. She doesn't always "leap" at the opportunity to hop on his finger anymore and must be prodded now and then. He succeeds by pushing his finger horizontally behind and toward her feet and then she BACKS on.

She would not sit for more than one picture today -- another show of independence. Usually it is we who have to remove her from the model's stand. Instead, she flitted and flew about examining the camera and tripod, daring us to restrain her.

She also seems to have examined EVERYTHING in the shop, for we find traces of her everywhere.

She was unsettled and refused to cooperate.

Preening.

JUNE 20. Robin left Sam's shoulder as he was passing through the house, flying wildly about the living room. She wanted to play tag and refused to be caught. Fortunately, the cat was in another part of the house, unaware of a potential dinner. As Robin was flying around dropping "things" on the upholstery, I pondered how we had managed to become surrogate parents to three different animals. We had inherited the cat, abandoned by former renters; the large white dog was a temporary but lengthy guest while our daughter adventured in the Yucatan; and now we had Robin -- temporary, too, yet she had already absorbed so much of our time and emotions we felt as if she had been with us a lifetime. Because of her vulnerability, Robin had to be kept safely isolated from the cat, the cat had to confined in the house away from the busy street, and the dog had to be kept away from the nasty temper of the cat. Precautions and arrangements for assured safety, individual playtime, and the care and feeding of each commanded a daily routine which we laughingly labeled the "Beastie shuffle."

Robin finally tired of her game of tag and allowed herself to be captured and things settled back to NORMAL again.

JUNE 21. Robin was enthralled with a big, luscious-looking store-bought California strawberry which we offered her, and she eagerly accepted the first bite, but then, strangely, clamped her mouth shut. Each time we tried to offer her another morsel, her beak seemed to close even tighter. Next, we offered her a red grape. Now, THAT was different! She repeatedly opened her mouth for more. When we tried to sneak in a piece of strawberry, she clamped her beak immediately. Had she become that discriminating about garden-fresh berries over store-bought ones? Our own

She clamped her mouth shut and glared at us.

64

berries had finished bearing, so we never had the opportunity to pursue the experiment further.

JUNE 22. Instead of following Robin to her feeding station this morning, Sam just stood in the doorway to see how she would react. When she realized that he wasn't responding to her demands, she ran back and leaped on the toe of his shoe! (Gosh, talk about winning ways.) When he started to move, she leaped off and raced toward her dining room again. Sam obligingly sat on the floor in his usual spot to feed her.

After a full meal and a short rest, she bathed. She did it with her usual vigor, then jumped into the dry dirt and onto Sam's knee. She allowed him the rare privilege of stroking her back while she stood perfectly still. Then he stroked some of the wing feathers individually and helped her remove portions of broken sheathing. It was a supreme moment in the life of a man with a wild bird.

Sam replenished the worms in the damp-earth box and noted Robin's response: she would look at the surface of the dirt straight-on with both eyes, seemingly noticing some movement in the dirt, then turn her head and focus on a spot with just one eye (she never followed through while we were in the room). Sam gave her some grapes and spent the rest of the morning puttering around his workbench with Robin at his side. He told me about it later in the day and how he finally had decided to give her up before she became any more dependent upon us.

We knew deep down that we must not keep her. Her freedom and best interests preyed on us constantly now, yet we didn't know exactly how and when to let go.

"Her tail is much longer now, over two inches," Sam remarked, knowing that TWO was the prescribed number. He called the bird woman again to report Robin's progress.

The woman said HER birds stay about six weeks. "Look for signs of independence. All robins become independent and start shying away from the protector-feeder, no matter how close the relationship has been. It is Nature taking over," she said. "Just don't release the bird in your neighborhood, when it's ready. It won't know enough to move quickly away from a cat."

Then, sensing his apprehensions about releasing Robin in the state park, she suggested we call Jack Eads, a man who nurses injured birds and cares for homeless ones. (He has a Federal license that permits him to work with creatures of the wild.) He has a type of transition home or half-way house consisting of sheltered flight pens in which birds are kept until they are well or have learned survival techniques. They learn to feed themselves by seeing others peck at seeds and grains -- this, of course, was the answer for Robin, who was without a role model and was approaching maturity. (Despite her secret midnight snack of worms, she still insisted on being fed with forceps.) Here at last was a solution which Sam and I both thought we might be able to accept.

Look for signs of independence.

67

Leaving Home and Hating It

JUNE 23. Reluctantly we made arrangements with Mr. Eads. Sam prepared a shoe box with paper towels, cut vents in the lid and sides. It was almost as if he were making a coffin. Holding back tears, he put Robin in it.

"She won't suffer injury in such a container -- she might do herself harm in something larger," Eads had instructed.

It was a sad day. My mother Selma, joined us as Sam and I made the fifteen-mile journey almost in silence as we all tried to hold back the tears. The slightest utterance from any of the three of us would have resulted in a quick cancellation of the trip. But we knew that parting was inevitable. If we turned around now, we would only have to repeat the whole ordeal tomorrow or the next day or the day after that. Robin fidgeted in the box and became progressively more restless. She hated barriers and enclosures. She couldn't understand the sudden confinement, refusing to be comforted even by Sam's voice which usually had a soothing effect on her. Maybe she was able to detect HIS feelings despite the soft-toned assurances.

I held the shoebox on my lap and peered at her through the vents. Her mouth was wide open. Was she going to be ill? Was she hot? Was she going to die? I put the box on the floor of the car, close to the cool-air vents, and hoped that would give her relief. Soon she quieted down. Eventually she closed her beak. Since then I have read that birds cool themselves by panting ". . . by evaporation of water from the inner surfaces of air sacs. The faster the bird breathes, the faster the cooling goes on."[12]

We arrived at the bird place and were encouraged to find a cool, lush green wooded area with covered holding-cages, perhaps ten in all, ranging from 4'x 6' to larger. Mr. Eads was cordial and patient as we talked and fussed over our Robin. Then, as if trying to create more understanding or empathy toward our orphan, we announced that our speckled, pale-breasted charge was female. (We had learned our conclusive information in our childhood readers: cock robins have a deep orange breast while hens are pale-breasted in order not to attract attention to the nest.)

"All first-year robins are speckled," Mr. Eads replied, "and it's difficult to tell whether they are male or female until the second year or so."

But we seemed to need a category for Robin. Besides, we were so accustomed to referring to her as "her," we justified it all by letting the degree of color on her speckled breast be the deciding factor.

Would she ever want to associate with other robins? We had hand-raised her -- had become her parents -- she loved US, trusted us, depended on us, -- now THIS. Perhaps it was a mistake to uproot her from her familiar, happy surroundings, from doting parents; perhaps we had been too much of an influence, to prevent her from making a successful transition to the world of birds. Mr. Eads, sensing our apprehensions, invited Sam to enter the cage with Robin still in her box.

The journey had been confining and foreign to her and now this: eight to ten birds all within reach and many more in adjacent flight pens -- she just wasn't accustomed to having other birds around. Only human companions. When Sam released her from the shoebox, she tried to fly in all directions at once. She flew from ground to perch and from perch to ground. She flew against the chicken-wire walls and tried to find a hole large enough to squeeze through. She clung to the wire and flapped her wings almost hysterically. She rebuffed Sam for bringing her to this god-awful madhouse. What fate had befallen her?

The aviary wasn't really a madhouse, but a calm, peaceful airy space. We were amazed with the unconcern of some of the birds and the friendliness of others. A tiny wax-wing, a sparrow, and three or four quail went about their quiet business pecking at things on the ground, bathing in the dirt, or socializing with one another -- and with us. One fat little robin leaped on Sam's hand and chattered insistently to him, then aimed its monologue at the rest of us through the fence.

"The sparrow over there was brought here as a baby with an injured leg. It has been well for a long time, but refuses to go away. It does leave the cage through holes in the mesh whenever it feels like it, but it always comes 'home' for the night," Mr. Eads remarked.

He assured us that Robin would adjust nicely and commended us for her good health and condition. He pointed to another robin, about her age, who seemed to be keeping an eye on her, and suggested to us the possibility of communication between the two. Robin did seem to be settling down a little. We assumed that the other robin was a male because of his deeper color. Perhaps he was telling her to relax -- that they'd have a great time together -- or that he was Head Honcho and NOBODY behaved like THAT in HIS territory.

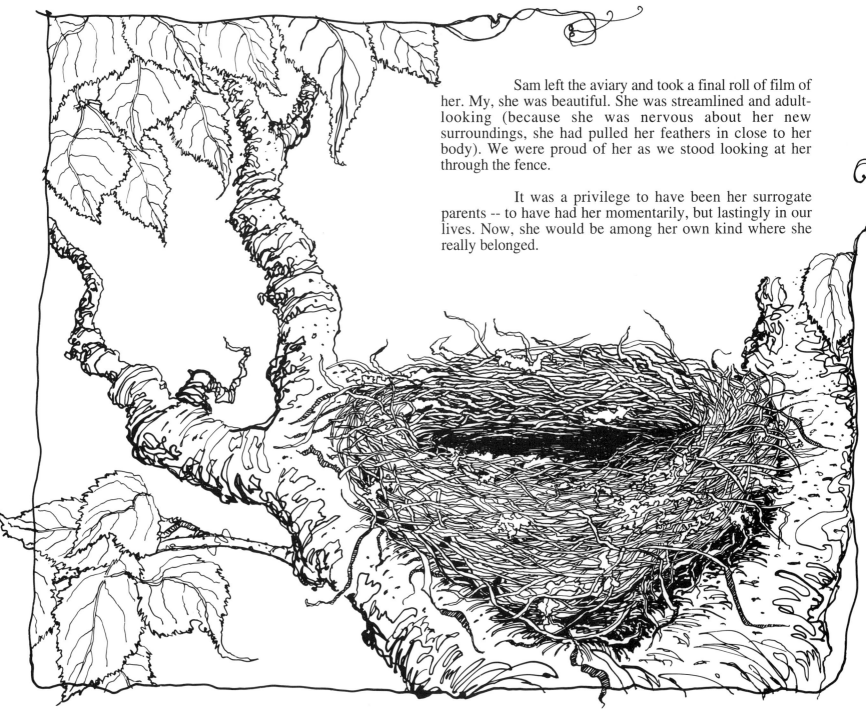

Sam left the aviary and took a final roll of film of her. My, she was beautiful. She was streamlined and adult-looking (because she was nervous about her new surroundings, she had pulled her feathers in close to her body). We were proud of her as we stood looking at her through the fence.

It was a privilege to have been her surrogate parents -- to have had her momentarily, but lastingly in our lives. Now, she would be among her own kind where she really belonged.

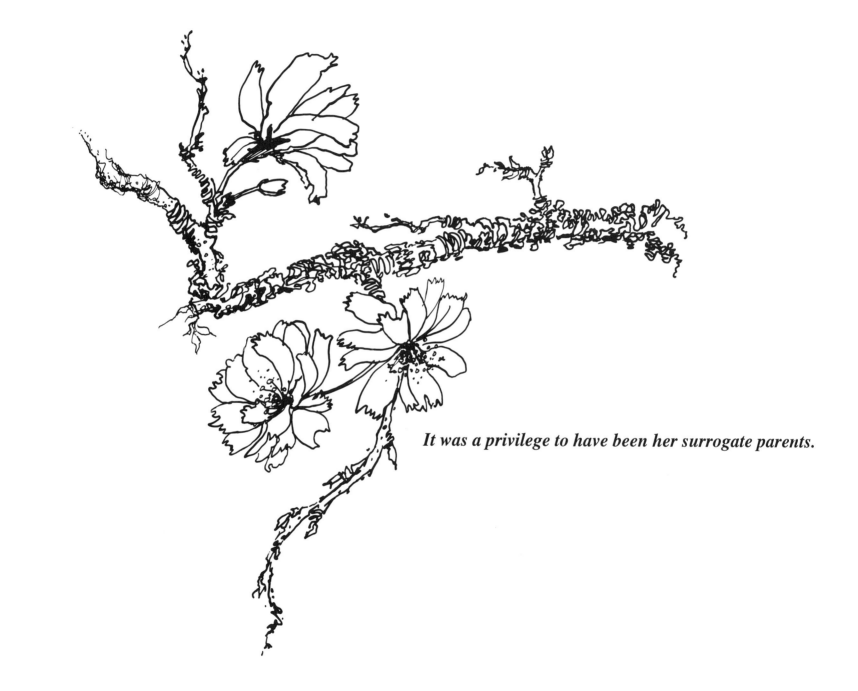

It was a privilege to have been her surrogate parents.

Epilogue

Sometime later we found Robert Hudson's *Nature's Nursery, Baby Birds,* in which he describes animal imprinting, the discovery of Dr. Konrad Lorenz, regarding the "critical periods of social development formation."

In birds, because of their rapid physical development, the critical period is short; "their social period is determined within a period lasting from the first two hours to, at the most, several days."[13] That information has given us considerable peace of mind and has muted our pain of having had to relinquish our Robin. She came to us between the 8th and 11th day after hatching (we never knew her order in the nest) -- well after the imprinting period by her biological parents -- and thereby had the capability of developing a normal social relationship in robindom.

It has been fifteen years now. The cherry blossoms still bloom each long winter's day and we still think about our baby bird. Our wonderful little "ROBIN-ROBIN". Does she continue to visit us each spring, or are those her children and grandchildren who keep coming to bring us joy and song? Whenever a robin lingers on the porch railing or stares at our bedroom window from a perch in the cherry tree our hearts skip a beat. Is it really you? Oh, how we long to touch you again -- our sweet lovely ROBIN-ROBIN!

Footnotes

1-David Lack, *The Life of the Robin* (London: H.F.& G. Witherby Ltd., 1944), p.87.

2-Geraldine Lux Flanagan and Sean Morris, *Window into a Nest* (Boston: Houghton Mifflin Company, 1975), p. 56.

3-Lack, 80.

4-Joan Carson, Ornithologist, telephone conversation, Poulsbo, Washington, October 30,1986.

5-Lack, 110.

6-Austin L. Rand, *Ornithology: an Introduction* (New York: W.W. Norton and Co., Inc., 1967), p. 180.

7-Joel Carl Welty, *The Life of Birds* (Philadelphia: W.B. Saunders Co., 1975), p. 32.

8-Rand, 43.

9-Welty, 77.

10-Rand, 44.

11-William L. Finley, "Robin," *Birds of America* (New York: Garden City Publishing Co., Inc., 1936), Part III, p. 236.

12-Rand, 72.

13-Robert G. Hudson, *Nature's Nursery, Baby Birds* (New York: The John Day Co., 1971), p.137.

Bibliography

Flanagan, Geraldine Lux and Morris, Sean. *Window into a Nest*. Boston: Houghton Mifflin Co., 1975.

Holden, Raymond P. *The Ways of Nesting Birds*. New York: Dodd, Mead, and Co., 1970.

Hudson, Robert G. *Nature's Nursery Baby Birds*. New York: The John Day Co., 1971.

Lack, David. *The Life of the Robin*. London: H.F.& G. Witherby Ltd., 1944.

Pearson, T. Gilbert, Editor-in-chief. *Birds of America*. New York: Garden City Pub. Co., 1936.

Peterson. Roger Tory. *A Field Guide to Western Birds*. Boston: Houghton Mifflin Company, 1941.

Rand, Austin L. *Ornithology: an Introduction*. New York: W.W. Norton and Co., Inc., 1967.

Terres, John K. *Songbirds in your Garden*. New York: Thomas Y. Crowell Company, 1953.

Welty, Joel Carl. *The Life of Birds*. Philadelphia: W.B. Saunders Company, 1975.

Other Sources

Ashenberg, Louise, Aide to Audubon Society, Consultations for maintenance of Robin, Tracyton, Washington, June 6 and 21, 1979.

Balcomb, Mary and Balcomb, Robert S., Daily Log, observation, and care of baby Robin. Silverdale, Washington, May 2, to June 23, 1979.

Carson, Joan, Ornithologist and journalist, Poulsbo, Washington. Telephone conversation, October 30, 1986.

Eads, Jack, licensed bird handler for Audubon Society. Port Orchard, Washington, June 23, 1979.

ZINA Age 4½

HAPPINESS IS: HEARING A
BIRD SING.

Design: Mary N. Balcomb
Design Consultant: Amis Balcomb
Production: Amis Balcomb
Etchings, drawings, photographs: Mary N. Balcomb
Studio photographs: Robert S. Balcomb
Printed and bound: BookCrafters, United States of America